Elizabeth I

Jane Bingham

Raintree

Chicago, Illinois

HEINEMANN·RAINTREE

TO ORDER:
☎ Phone Customer Service **888-454-2279**
💻 Visit **www.heinemannraintree.com** to browse our catalog and order online.

© 2009 Raintree
a division of Pearson Inc.
Chicago, Illinois

Customer Service 888-454-2279
Visit our website at www.heinemannraintree.com

Edited by Louise Galpine and Catherine Clarke
Designed by Kimberly R. Miracle, Jennifer Lacki,
 and Betsy Wernert
Original illustrations © Pearson Education Limited
Illustrations by Mapping Specialists
Picture research by Hannah Taylor and Helen Reilly

Originated by Modern Age
Printed in China by Leo Paper Group

ISBN-13: 978-1-4109-3219-8 (hc)
ISBN-10: 1-4109-3219-2 (hc)

13 12 11 10 09
10 9 8 7 6 5 4 3 2 1

Library of Congress Cataloging-in-Publication Data
Bingham, Jane.
 Elizabeth I/ Jane Bingham.
  p. cm. -- (Great women leaders)
 Includes bibliographical references and index.
 ISBN 978-1-4109-3219-8 (hc)
 1. Elizabeth I, Queen of England, 1533-1603--Juvenile
literature. 2. Great Britain--History--Elizabeth, 1558-1603-
-Juvenile literature. 3. Queens--Great Britain--Biography--
Juvenile literature. I. Title.
 DA355.B58 2008
 942.05'5'092--dc22

                                2007049815

Acknowledgments
The publishers would like to thank the following for permission
to reproduce photographs: © akg-images **pp. 6** (Nimatallah),
11 (Bildarchiv Monheim), **12** (Erich Lessing), **38** (Sotheby's),
39; © The Art Archive (Palazzo Pitti Florence/Dagli Orti) **p. 4**; ©
The Bridgeman Art Library **pp. 7** (Giraudon/Galleria Nazionale
de Capodimonte, Naples, Italy), **8** (Hever Castle Ltd, Kent, UK),
15 (Trustees of the Bedford Estate, Woburn Abbey, UK), **17**
(Giraudon/Prado, Madrid, Spain), **18** (National Portrait Gallery,
London, UK), **19** (National Portrait Gallery, London, UK), **21**
(Private Collection/The Stapleton Collection), **23** (The Royal
Cornwall Museum, Truro, Cornwall, UK), **25** (Private Collection/
Richard Philip, London), **27** (Scottish National Portrait Gallery,
Edinburgh, Scotland), **29** (Private Collection/The Stapleton
Collection), **30** (Woburn Abbey, Bedfordshire, UK), **31** (Private
Collection/Rafael Valls Gallery, London, UK), **33** (The Crown
Estate), **34** (Private Collection), **35** (British Library, London,
UK/British Library Board), **36** (Guildhall Library, City of London),
37 (Private Collection), **41** (Prado, Madrid, Spain); © Corbis **pp.**
16 (Douglas Pearson), **40** (Angelo Hornak); © National Portrait
Gallery (London) **p. 32**; © Photolibrary (Robert Harding Picture
Library) **pp. 9, 20**; © The Royal Collection/Her Majesty Queen
Elizabeth II **p. 10**; © TopFoto/Roger-Viollet **p. 24**.

Cover photograph of Queen Elizabeth I in her coronation robes
reproduced with permission of © Corbis (Fine Art Photographic
Library).

We would like to thank Nancy Harris for her invaluable help in
the preparation of this book.

Every effort has been made to contact copyright holders of
material reproduced in this book. Any omissions will be rectified
in subsequent printings if notice is given to the publishers.

CONTENTS

Some words are shown in bold, **like this**. You can find out what they mean by looking in the glossary.

ELIZABETH, QUEEN OF ENGLAND

In 1558 a small, redheaded woman was crowned queen of England. She was just 25 years old. Nobody guessed that she would become one of England's greatest rulers.

For the next 45 years, Queen Elizabeth I ruled alone. When she died, England was a peaceful and powerful nation.

This is a portrait of Queen Elizabeth that was painted when she was still alive.

A Tudor queen

Elizabeth was the last of the Tudor rulers. The Tudor family ruled England for more than 100 years. They included:

Henry VII (Elizabeth's grandfather): Ruled 1485–1509

Henry VIII (Elizabeth's father): Ruled 1509–1547

Edward VI (Elizabeth's half-brother): Ruled 1547–1553

Mary I (Elizabeth's half-sister): Ruled 1553–1558

Elizabeth I: Ruled 1558–1603.

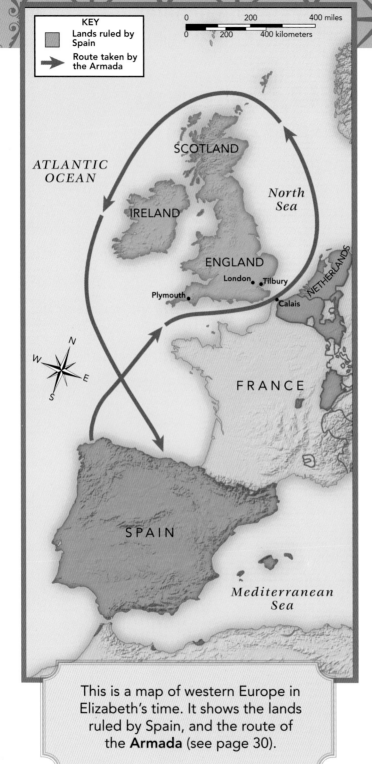

This is a map of western Europe in Elizabeth's time. It shows the lands ruled by Spain, and the route of the **Armada** (see page 30).

An exciting reign

Elizabeth faced many difficulties. She survived **plots** against her life. She fought off an **invasion** from Spain. She also sent explorers and traders all over the world.

While Queen Elizabeth was on the throne, many people in England became richer. It was also a great time for musicians, artists, and writers. Later, people saw Elizabeth's **reign** as a glorious period in English history. They called this time the Elizabethan age.

A strong woman

Queen Elizabeth never married. She proved that a woman could rule alone. Elizabeth was loved and feared by her people. But most of all she was admired.

KING HENRY'S DAUGHTER

On September 7, 1533, a princess was born. She was the daughter of the king of England, Henry VIII, and his new wife, Anne Boleyn. Her royal parents named their daughter Elizabeth.

A girl, not a boy

When Elizabeth was born, King Henry was very disappointed. He wanted a son to be the next king. At that time, everyone thought that men made better rulers than women. Henry had planned a great celebration to welcome his new son. Now he canceled all his plans.

This is a portrait of Henry VIII, painted in Tudor times.

A second daughter

Elizabeth was Henry's second daughter. Henry had married Catherine of Aragon when he was 18. Catherine had given birth to a daughter named Mary. Then, Catherine had one more daughter, but the baby died. Henry was desperate for a son.

In 1533 Henry **divorced** Catherine of Aragon and married Anne Boleyn. He hoped his new wife would give him the son whom he longed for.

Henry's divorce

Henry wanted to divorce Catherine so he could marry again. But divorce was forbidden by the **Catholic Church**. Henry asked the **pope** (the head of the Catholic Church) for special permission. When the pope refused, Henry was furious. He left the Catholic Church and created the **Church of England**. Then, he went ahead and divorced Catherine.

In Tudor times, the pope was seen as more powerful than any king. This painting shows Pope Clement VII.

Princess Elizabeth

Elizabeth was sent off to live in the country when she
was still a baby. Meanwhile, Henry and Anne stayed in
London. After that, Elizabeth rarely saw her parents. She
was brought up by **noblewomen**, who dressed her in
fine clothes and played with her.

Henry and Anne

Henry had fallen in love with Anne Boleyn when she was
a **lady-in-waiting** at the royal **court**. But their marriage
was not a success. They both had fiery tempers, and
Anne did not give birth to a son. After only three years
of marriage, Henry decided it was time for a change. He
gave orders for Anne to be **executed**.

Death of a mother

Elizabeth was nearly three
years old when Anne was
killed. Later, she refused to
talk about her mother, but
she is thought to have worn
a picture of Anne in a
special ring.

This is a portrait of Henry's wife
and Elizabeth's mother,
Anne Boleyn.

King Henry's wives

After Anne Boleyn died, King Henry VIII married four more times. His third wife was Jane Seymour, who died after giving birth to a son. Next, Henry married Anne of Cleves, but he quickly **divorced** her and married Catherine Howard. In 1542 Henry gave orders for Catherine Howard to be executed. Then, he married his last wife, Catherine Parr. Altogether, he had six wives.

Henry VIII caused great resentment by getting rid of the **Catholic monasteries**. The monasteries fell into ruins, and some of them are still ruins today.

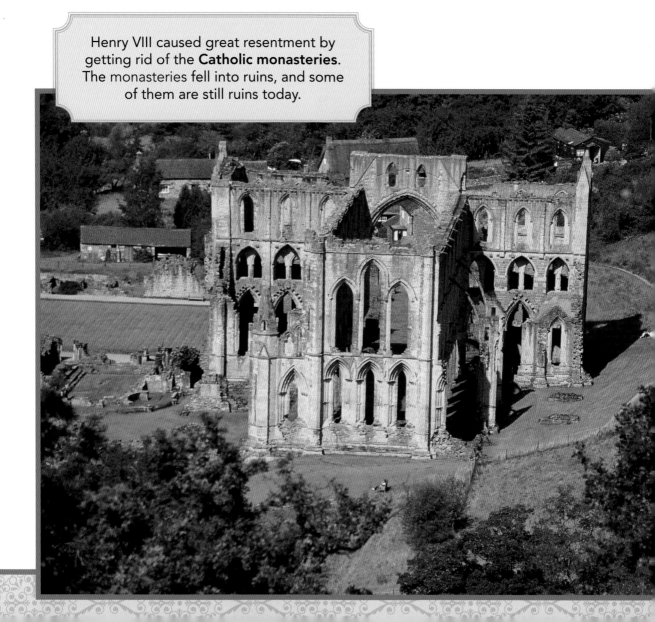

A Country Childhood

After Anne Boleyn had been **executed**, Elizabeth was no longer a royal princess. Instead, she was known as Lady Elizabeth. She lived a quiet life in Hatfield House, about 30 miles (48 kilometers) north of London.

Lady Elizabeth

The young Lady Elizabeth had many servants to take care of her. She also had a **governess** to help with her studies. In addition to learning to read and write, Elizabeth learned to sing, dance, and play music. She spent a lot of time outdoors, riding her horse and hunting with hawks.

This painting shows Elizabeth when she was about 13 years old.

Elizabeth and Mary lived at Hatfield House.

Mary and Elizabeth

King Henry's oldest daughter, Mary, also lived at Hatfield House. Even though Mary was 13 years older than Elizabeth, the girls were friends. Mary taught Elizabeth to play cards.

Mary and Elizabeth spent a lot of time together, but there was one major difference between them. Mary was a **Catholic** and Elizabeth was a **Protestant** (see box). Many Catholics saw the Protestants as their enemies. Later, this caused serious problems for Elizabeth.

Protestants and Catholics

In the 1500s there were two main religions in Europe: the Catholic Church, which was led by the **pope** in Rome, and the Protestant Church. The Protestants had broken away from the Catholic Church and did not recognize the pope as their leader. Members of King Henry VIII's **Church of England** were Protestants.

This is a portrait of
Edward VI, Elizabeth's
half-brother.

A prince is born

When Elizabeth was four years old, King Henry finally had a son. His third wife, Jane Seymour, gave birth to Edward. Sadly, Jane died 12 days later. Now, Elizabeth was third in line to the throne, behind her younger brother, Edward, and her older sister, Mary. There seemed little chance that she would ever be queen.

Edward and Elizabeth

Elizabeth loved her half-brother, Edward. They were both brought up as **Protestants** and often studied together. Edward was a very intelligent boy, but he was often sick. He admired his sister Elizabeth very much.

Henry dies

King Henry died in 1547. Elizabeth was 13 years old. When she heard the news, Elizabeth wept briefly, but she quickly recovered.

Elizabeth had never been close to her father because he was always busy at **court**. But in many ways they were alike. Henry and Elizabeth were both strong characters, and they each had a very quick temper. They loved music, dancing, and outdoor sports such as hunting and archery (shooting arrows at targets).

Boys before girls

In Tudor times boys had the right to rule before girls. When a king died, his oldest son was the next in line to the throne. This meant that the oldest son would automatically be the next person to rule the country. If the oldest child in a royal family was a girl, her brother would still rule before her.

ELIZABETH IN DANGER

After King Henry died, nine-year-old Edward became King Edward VI of England. During his **reign** Elizabeth spent most of her time in the country.

Six years after he came to the throne, Edward died from tuberculosis (a serious lung disease). Mary was crowned Queen Mary I of England shortly after this.

A Catholic queen

Queen Mary was determined to make England into a **Catholic** country once again. To help her in her task, she decided to marry a Catholic. Mary chose Philip, the only son of the king of Spain. This was a very unpopular choice. Many people feared that the Spanish prince would take control of England.

Protestant protest

The English **Protestants** hated the idea of a Catholic queen, and they wanted Elizabeth to rule instead. When Mary announced her plans to marry Philip of Spain, a Protestant **nobleman** led a **rebellion** against her. The rebellion failed and the nobleman was captured. He was later **executed**. But Mary was still angry. She thought Elizabeth had helped to plan the rebellion.

This Tudor portrait shows Queen Mary with Philip of Spain.

Spanish power

In Elizabeth's time, Spain was the richest and most powerful country in the world. The king of Spain ruled vast areas of land in South America. Ships full of silver and gold sailed from the Americas to Spain.

The Tower of London was used to imprison enemies of the king or queen.

Locked in the tower

Elizabeth told Mary that she knew nothing about the **rebellion**, but Mary wasn't taking any chances. She gave orders that Elizabeth should be locked in the Tower of London. The Tower was England's most terrifying prison. Most people who entered it never came out alive.

Elizabeth spent two months in the Tower before Mary decided to set her free. Then, she was taken to a small palace near Oxford, in England. Mary insisted that Elizabeth should stay in the palace for the next year.

A troubled reign

Queen Mary had a short and troubled **reign**. Even though she married Prince Philip of Spain, they did not have any children. She also failed to turn England into a **Catholic** country. In 1558 Mary died, and Philip returned to Spain. Now it was Elizabeth's turn to rule.

Elizabeth is queen

Elizabeth was at Hatfield House when she heard the news that her sister had died and so she was now queen. She set off on a grand procession to London and was welcomed by cheering crowds. But not everyone was pleased that she was queen. There were many challenges ahead.

When Mary (below) was queen, she imprisoned her sister Elizabeth because she feared a rebellion.

These are Elizabeth's words, when she heard the news that she was queen of England:

"This is God's doing; it is marvelous in our eyes."

THE NEW QUEEN

Elizabeth was crowned Queen Elizabeth I of England in January 1559. The day before her **coronation** she was carried through the streets of London in an open carriage.

After she had been crowned, a very grand feast was held in her honor. It was a dramatic start to the young queen's **reign**.

This painting shows Elizabeth in her coronation robes.

Elizabeth in charge

At first, people worried that a young woman of 25 could not rule England on her own. But Elizabeth soon showed that she was in charge. At the first meeting of her **advisors**, she announced that she expected all her people to obey her.

Elizabeth also insisted that everyone at the royal **court** show her great respect. No one was allowed to sit when she was standing. Anyone who spoke to the queen had to kneel on one knee.

Taking advice

Elizabeth held meetings with her advisors every day. She also took the advice of **Parliament**. This was a group of men who had been chosen to represent the English people. Elizabeth was very intelligent and enjoyed the challenge of ruling well.

Sir William Cecil was Elizabeth's chief advisor. He served the queen for 40 years.

Only the best

Elizabeth liked to be surrounded by good-looking people. There is a story that she once refused to employ a young man because he had a front tooth missing!

Many homes

As queen, Elizabeth owned many palaces and homes. During the winter she spent most of her time in Whitehall Palace in London. During the summer she visited her country homes. One of her favorite homes was Hampton Court Palace. The palace was about 10 miles (16 kilometers) from the center of London, on the bank of the Thames River.

Elizabeth's court

Wherever she traveled, Elizabeth was surrounded by her royal **court**. The court was made up partly of Elizabeth's friends, **advisors**, and servants. All these people were known as the queen's **courtiers**.

Elizabeth's father, King Henry VIII, rebuilt Hampton Court Palace.

Elizabeth was carried in an open carriage, surrounded by servants.

Many others came to court just to see the queen. Sometimes as many as 10,000 people gathered in the royal palaces for a special event such as a dance.

Royal tours

Elizabeth knew that it was very important to be seen by her people. She made special journeys all over England. She was carried in an open carriage at the head of a grand procession. Behind the queen came her courtiers, riding on horseback, and her servants, walking on foot. They were followed by many covered wagons filled with Elizabeth's dresses and jewelry.

Entertaining the queen

When Queen Elizabeth toured her kingdom, she usually stayed the night with a **noble** family. It was very expensive having the queen as a guest. The families who welcomed Elizabeth had to look after all her courtiers and servants as well. Often there were 1,000 people to feed.

A husband for the queen?

Everyone at **court** expected Elizabeth to marry. Even though she was a strong ruler, people still thought she needed a husband. They also thought the queen should have children, to provide an **heir** to the throne. But Elizabeth was not in a hurry to find a husband.

When Elizabeth was asked in **Parliament** when she was going to marry, she replied:

"I am already bound unto a husband, which is the kingdom of England."

Foreign suitors

Many powerful men offered to marry Elizabeth. She had offers of marriage from Philip of Spain and from royal princes in Sweden and France.

Elizabeth took her time to respond to these offers. She had to decide if she really wanted England to be linked to another country. For a long time, she kept her admirers guessing. Then, she refused them all.

Sweet Robin

Elizabeth was very fond of an English **nobleman** named Robert Dudley. She had known Dudley since she was eight, and she sometimes called him "sweet Robin." But Dudley had a wife, so he could not marry the queen.

Some people think that Elizabeth never married because she was in love with Robert Dudley. Others think she made a choice to stay single. They believe Elizabeth got used to ruling alone, and she did not want to share her power.

Elizabeth and Dudley liked
to play music together.

Plots Against the Queen

As soon as Elizabeth became queen, she announced that England was a **Protestant** country. This made the English **Catholics** very unhappy. Some of them even wanted to kill Elizabeth and replace her with a Catholic ruler.

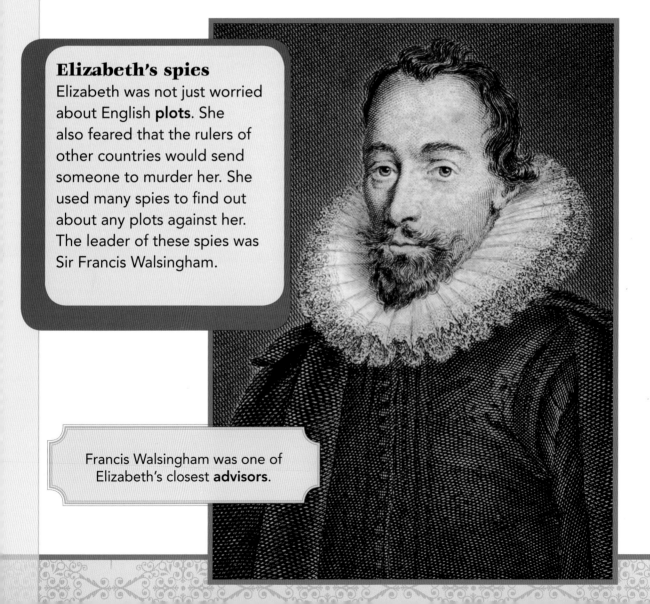

Elizabeth's spies
Elizabeth was not just worried about English **plots**. She also feared that the rulers of other countries would send someone to murder her. She used many spies to find out about any plots against her. The leader of these spies was Sir Francis Walsingham.

Francis Walsingham was one of Elizabeth's closest **advisors**.

Mary Stuart, Queen of Scots

Many English Catholics wanted Mary Stuart (often called Mary, Queen of Scots) to be their queen. Mary was Elizabeth's cousin, and a Catholic. For a while, she was queen of Scotland. But then the Scots turned against her because they did not trust the man she had married. They made her son, James, the new Scottish king, and captured Mary.

Mary in England

In 1568 Mary escaped to England and asked Elizabeth to protect her. This put Elizabeth in a very difficult situation. She was afraid that if Mary lived freely in England, she could lead a Catholic **rebellion** and try to replace Elizabeth as queen.

Mary was kept a prisoner in English castles for 19 years.

Elizabeth decided it was far too dangerous for her cousin Mary to be free. She gave orders that Mary should be kept as a prisoner. Elizabeth also made sure that Mary lived in comfort, however, with servants to take care of her.

Early plots

Soon after Mary Stuart arrived in England, there were two attempts to make her queen. In 1569 some **Catholic noblemen** in the north of England led a **rebellion** against Elizabeth. They claimed that Mary was the true queen of England, but their rebellion was soon defeated.

Two years later, another Catholic nobleman tried to free Mary from prison. He was captured and **executed**, but Elizabeth did not have Mary killed. There was no proof that Mary knew about the **plot**, so Elizabeth refused to punish her.

The Babington plot

In 1586 Mary was finally caught plotting against Elizabeth. The plot was organized by an English nobleman, Sir Anthony Babington. It also involved King Philip of Spain. This time Elizabeth realized she would have to take firm action.

Mary's death

Elizabeth was very unhappy about putting Mary to death, but **Parliament** persuaded her it had to be done. In 1587 she gave orders for Mary to be executed. Six months after the execution, Elizabeth ordered a grand funeral for her cousin. She wanted to show proper respect to another queen.

MARIA
D G
SCOTIÆ
PIISSIMA REGINA
FRANCIÆ DOTARIA
ANNO
ÆTATIS REGNIQ
36
ANGLICÆ CAPTIVIT
10
S H
1578

This portrait shows Mary, Queen of Scots, when she was around 35 years old. Mary was executed 10 years after this, in 1587.

A hard decision

The day that Mary died, Elizabeth refused to see anyone and sent away her food. She would not even talk to her trusted **advisor**, Sir William Cecil. Elizabeth hated the thought of a queen being executed. It reminded her too much of her father's **reign**, when two queens (including Elizabeth's mother) were executed.

ELIZABETH AT WAR

Elizabeth's great enemy was King Philip of Spain. Philip was a **devout Catholic** who hated the fact that England was a **Protestant** country. He also had other reasons for hating Elizabeth.

Raids at sea

Spain owned vast areas of land in South America. This meant that many Spanish ships crossed the Atlantic Ocean, sailing from South America to Spain. The ships were filled with treasure such as silver and gold. Elizabeth saw the chance to steal this treasure for England.

Elizabeth sent daring sea captains into the Atlantic to trade and explore. But the captains also attacked the Spanish ships and stole their treasure. When Philip protested about these attacks, Elizabeth said there was nothing she could do to stop them. This made Philip furious.

Philip and Elizabeth

Before he became king of Spain, Philip had been married to Elizabeth's half-sister Mary. When Mary died, Philip offered to marry Elizabeth, so that he could keep control of England. Elizabeth refused Philip's offer of marriage, and gradually the two rulers became enemies.

Sir John Hawkins was a bold sea captain who was hated by the Spanish.

Time to attack

In 1585 Elizabeth upset the Spanish again. She sent some English troops to support the Netherlands in their war against Spain. Two years later, Mary, Queen of Scots, was **executed**. Philip was shocked by the death of a Catholic queen. He decided it was time to **invade** England.

Preparing for war

In 1588 about 130 ships set off from Spain. This massive **fleet** was known as the Spanish **Armada**. Meanwhile, in England, Elizabeth prepared for war. She gathered an army at Tilbury and a fleet of about 150 ships at Plymouth (see map on page 5). Then, the English waited for the Spanish ships to arrive.

On July 29 the Armada reached the French **port** of Calais. Here, the Spanish rested for the night before they crossed the English Channel to attack England. However, the English **navy** had another plan. It decided to surprise the Armada.

This portrait of Elizabeth shows the ships of the Armada behind her.

In this painting, English fire ships are being sent toward the Spanish fleet.

Battle begins

At midnight, the English sent eight fire ships toward the Armada. Fire ships were empty wooden ships that had been set on fire. The blazing ships caused a lot of damage to the Armada. Several Spanish ships burst into flames.

Later, the two fleets fought a battle at sea. There was no clear winner, but the Armada was greatly weakened. Then, a violent storm arrived. Powerful winds blew the Spanish ships out of the English Channel. England was now out of danger.

The end of the Armada

Driven by storms, the Armada was forced to sail all the way around the British Isles. Many Spanish ships were wrecked, and the remaining fleet returned to Spain. Elizabeth had won a victory against Spain.

Bowls or battle?

One of the leading captains of the English fleet was Sir Francis Drake. He always stayed very calm in battle. When the Armada was sighted, Drake was playing a game of **bowls**. He calmly finished the game before he returned to his ship.

GOOD QUEEN BESS

After the defeat of the Spanish **Armada**, people in England felt much safer than before. They felt very proud of Elizabeth, and they gave her the name "Good Queen Bess." In the course of her long **reign**, Good Queen Bess made her country great in many ways.

This famous portrait shows Elizabeth standing on a map of the world.

Sir Francis Drake had many adventures. He even explored the Antarctic Ocean.

Exploring the world

During Elizabeth's reign, England was famous for its explorers. The queen paid for many daring **voyages** to discover new land. Martin Frobisher reached northern Canada, and Humphrey Gilbert claimed Newfoundland for his queen.

Francis Drake was the most famous Elizabethan explorer. He sailed all the way around the world in his ship, the *Golden Hind*. When Drake returned, Elizabeth made him a knight, giving him the title Sir Francis Drake.

Settling in North America

Another explorer, Sir Walter Raleigh, made the first English voyage to North America. He landed on the east coast of North America and called the place where he landed "Virginia." The other people with Raleigh tried to live in Virginia for a while. However, they found the life very hard and did not stay long.

Gifts from new lands

Sir Walter Raleigh was a great favorite of Elizabeth's. There is a famous story that he brought two gifts for her from the Americas. According to the story, Raleigh presented Elizabeth with potatoes and tobacco. Nobody knows if this is true.

Shakespeare's plays were performed at the Globe Theater in London.

Poetry and plays

Elizabeth was very proud of the talents of her people. She encouraged writers, artists, and musicians. Poets came to her **court** to read her their works. **Playwrights** performed their latest plays in front of the queen.

The greatest writer of Elizabeth's time was William Shakespeare. It is believed that some of Shakespeare's plays were written specifically to please the queen.

Marvelous music

Queen Elizabeth was very musical. In addition to singing and dancing, she played the lute (a kind of early guitar). She also played the virginals (a keyboard instrument).

During Elizabeth's **reign**, **composers** wrote great music for church services. They also composed madrigals, which were songs with different parts for high and low voices.

Fantastic fashions

Elizabeth thought it was very important to dress magnificently. She also expected everyone else at court to dress well. Elizabeth had more than 250 dresses made from velvet, satin, and silk. She wore dazzling jewelry and even had jewels and pearls in her hair.

Smelly court

People at Elizabeth's court dressed very fashionably, but they did not smell very nice. In Elizabethan times, even very wealthy people rarely took a bath, and their clothes were not often washed. Some people carried a fruit stuffed with **cloves**. They hoped the strong smell of the cloves would disguise the other smells!

At Elizabeth's court, musicians played while people ate.

Encouraging trade

Elizabeth recognized that trade was very important for her country. She encouraged **merchants** to find new markets for their goods. During her **reign**, English merchants began to trade in the Americas. Traders also traveled to new areas of Africa and Asia. By the time Elizabeth died, England was a wealthy nation.

A growing city

The city of London grew very fast in Elizabethan times. London had some expensive houses and gardens, but it also had many crowded buildings and narrow streets. The Thames River ran through the center of London. London Bridge was the only crossing place, but there were many barges to carry people across the river.

St. Paul's Church (at the top of this picture) was a famous landmark of the Elizabethan city of London.

Helping the poor

In Elizabeth's time, there was not enough food to feed everyone in England. Some people even starved to death. Elizabeth made the rich pay taxes (money for the government). She used this money to help support the poor and to build **workhouses**. Workhouses were places where very poor people could live and work.

Rich and poor

In Elizabethan times, the rich and poor had very different lives. Wealthy people lived in enormous homes with many servants. They ate at huge banquets and dressed in fine clothes. Poor people lived in very small cottages or had no homes at all. Their main food was bread or porridge, and they wore simple clothes or rags. Many poor people had no shoes, even in winter.

Beggars and other poor people were a common sight in Elizabethan England. This beggar is being dragged through the streets.

The End of a Golden Age

Elizabeth ruled England until her death, at the age of 69. She stayed fairly fit, but the last years of her **reign** were hard for her. Most of her friends had died, and she was very lonely.

Wigs and makeup

Elizabeth hated looking old, and she tried to hide the signs of old age. She wore very thick makeup, which made her look extremely pale. She also covered her thinning hair with a bright red wig.

As she grew older, Elizabeth tried very hard to look young and beautiful.

Losing Dudley

As Elizabeth grew older, the person she missed most was Robert Dudley. He was probably her closest friend, and she trusted his advice. Dudley died at the time of the Spanish **Armada**, when Elizabeth was around 55 years old. She never recovered from his death. She kept his last letter by her bed for the rest of her life.

Elizabeth and Essex

In the last years of her reign, Elizabeth spent a lot of time with a handsome young **nobleman** known as the Earl of Essex.

Elizabeth gave the Earl of Essex a lot of power, but that just made him hungry for more. Around 1600 he led a **rebellion** against the queen. The rebellion was a failure, and Essex was **executed**. Elizabeth was very sad that her favorite had turned against her. Now she felt even more alone.

The Earl of Essex was young and greedy for power.

Death of a queen

In her final years, Elizabeth often suffered from toothaches, but she refused to have her teeth pulled out. She also started to go blind and her memory began to fail.

In February 1603 Elizabeth caught a fever, and a few weeks later she died. She was given a magnificent funeral at Westminster Abbey in London.

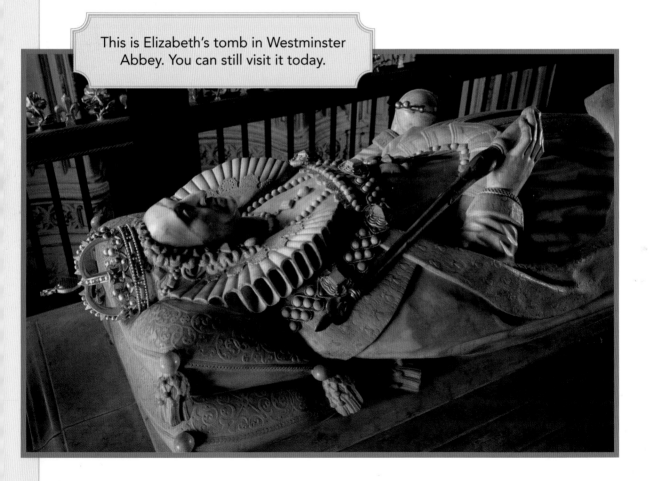

This is Elizabeth's tomb in Westminster Abbey. You can still visit it today.

Who will be next?

Because Elizabeth had no children, she had to choose England's next ruler. But she always refused to name her **successor**. Finally, she chose King James VI of Scotland. James was the son of Mary, Queen of Scots. He was a **Protestant** and a member of the Stuart family.

James was crowned King James I of England. The **reign** of the Tudor family had come to an end, and a new line of Stuart rulers had begun.

A golden age

After Elizabeth's death, people saw her reign as a "golden age." They recognized all the things she had done to make her country great. In her long reign, Elizabeth had proved that a woman could be a strong and **inspiring** leader.

James I was the new king of England.

Throughout her life, Elizabeth was eager to show that women could be just as good as men. At the time of the Spanish **Armada**, she told her army:

"I have but the body of a weak and feeble woman, but I have the heart and stomach of a king."

TIMELINES

Elizabeth's life

1533   Elizabeth is born

1536   Anne Boleyn (Elizabeth's mother) is **executed**

1547   King Henry VIII dies. Edward VI becomes king.

1553   King Edward VI dies. Lady Jane Grey **reigns** for just nine days. Mary I becomes queen.

1554   A **Protestant nobleman** named Sir Thomas Wyatt leads a **rebellion** against Queen Mary

1558   Queen Mary I dies. Elizabeth I becomes queen.

1568   Elizabeth imprisons Mary, Queen of Scots

1569   The first Protestant rebellion against Elizabeth is defeated

1580   Sir Francis Drake returns from his **voyage** around the world

1584   Sir Walter Raleigh claims Virginia, in North America, for Elizabeth

1585   Elizabeth sends troops to support the Netherlands in a war against Spain

1586   The Babington **plot** against Elizabeth is discovered

1587   Mary, Queen of Scots, is executed

1588   The Spanish **Armada** is defeated. Robert Dudley dies.

1598   William Cecil dies

1601   The Earl of Essex is executed, after his rebellion against the queen fails

1603   Queen Elizabeth I dies. James I becomes king.

World timeline

1521   Spanish troops **conquer** the Aztec people and take control of Mexico

1526   Babur becomes the first Mughal emperor of India

1535   Spanish troops conquer the Inca Empire and take control of Peru, in South America

1543   Andreas Vesalius, from Brussels, is the first person to make a detailed study of the human body

1547   Tsar Ivan IV (known as Ivan the Terrible) starts to rule in Russia

1562   England joins the slave trade, shipping slaves from Africa to the Americas

1564   William Shakespeare is born

1566   The Turkish Ottoman Empire reaches its largest size

1600   The East India Company is created in England, to trade with India

1600   The Oyo kingdom in West Africa is at its height

GLOSSARY

advisor someone who gives helpful advice. Elizabeth had many advisors who helped her to make some difficult decisions.

armada very large number of ships. The Spanish Armada included around 150 ships.

bowls game played with large, heavy balls on a flat, grassy surface

Catholic someone who belongs to a branch of the Christian Church that is led by the pope in Rome. Catholics are sometimes also known as Roman Catholics.

Church of England branch of the Christian religion. The Church of England is sometimes called the Anglican Church.

cloves dried, unopened buds of the clove tree, which are used as a strong-smelling spice

composer someone who writes music. Beethoven was a famous composer.

conquer defeat an enemy and take control of them by force

coronation religious service in which a new king or queen is crowned. Elizabeth I's coronation was held in 1558.

court people, including advisors and servants, who gather around a ruler. The court usually gathers in a royal palace.

courtier someone who is close to a ruler and is an important figure at the royal court. Queen Elizabeth I liked to be surrounded by courtiers.

devout very focused on religion. Devout Christians spend a lot of time praying and going to church.

divorce legal end of a marriage

execute kill someone as punishment for a crime

fleet large number of ships. A fleet is usually smaller than an armada.

governess woman who teaches children in their own home. Today, it is very unusual for children to have a governess.

heir person who will receive money, land, or a job when his or her parents die. When Henry VIII died, Prince Edward became king because he was heir to the British throne.

inspiring encouraging another person to do something by setting a good example. Baseball stars inspire young players to practice harder.

invasion when soldiers are sent into another country in order to take it over

lady-in-waiting woman who helps to take care of a queen. Queen Elizabeth I had ladies-in-waiting help her put on her clothes and arrange her hair.

merchant someone who trades with foreign countries. In Tudor times, merchants traveled long distances by ship.

monastery group of buildings where monks live and work. Buddhists, Hindus, and Christians have monasteries.

navy ships and sailors that fight for a country at sea. In Tudor times England had a powerful navy.

noble person who has a very high rank in society. Males with this rank are called noblemen, and women with this rank are called noblewomen.

parliament group of people who make the laws of the country. Members of parliament represent the people and are voted for in an election.

playwright someone who writes plays. William Shakespeare is one of the world's most famous playwrights.

plot secret plan. Sometimes people make plots to kill an enemy.

pope leader of the Catholic Church. The pope lives in Rome.

port town with a harbor. Ships stop in ports to unload their goods and passengers.

Protestant someone who belongs to a branch of the Christian Church that does not have the pope as its leader. Protestants broke away from the Catholic Church in the 1500s.

rebellion violent protest against a ruler or a government. There were three major rebellions during Elizabeth's reign.

reign period of time during which a king or queen rules. The reign of Queen Elizabeth I lasted for 45 years.

successor person who takes over a job when somebody dies or stops working

voyage journey by sea. You can go on a voyage on a sailboat or on an ocean liner.

workhouse place where poor people worked in return for food and shelter. There were workhouses in Great Britain until the 1800s.

Want to Know More?

Books

Adams, Simon. *World History Biographies: Elizabeth I, the Outcast Who Became England's Queen.* Washington, D.C.: National Geographic Children's, 2005.

Simpson, Margaret. *Horribly Famous: Elizabeth I and Her Conquests.* New York: Scholastic, 2006.

Stanley, Diane, and Peter Vennema. *Good Queen Bess: The Story of Elizabeth I of England.* New York: Harper Collins, 2001.

Websites

http://tudorhistory.org/elizabeth
This site has a biography of Elizabeth, illustrated with lots of paintings.

www.bbc.co.uk/history/historic_figures/elizabeth_i_queen.shtml
This site covers many aspects of Elizabeth's reign. It includes a spying game and a view inside an Elizabethan room.

www.tudorbritain.org
A fun site about Tudor life, with lots of activities.

Places to visit

Fotheringhay Castle, Northamptonshire, England
The place where Mary, Queen of Scots, was executed.

Hatfield House, Hertfordshire, England
Elizabeth's childhood home.

Westminster Abbey, London, England
Tombs of Elizabeth I and Mary, Queen of Scots.

Tower of London, London, England
The prison where the young Elizabeth was held.

National Portrait Gallery, London, England
This gallery contains many portraits of famous Tudors.

INDEX